TOUGH QUESTION

**4**

# TOUGH QUESTIONS

# HOW COULD GOD ALLOW SUFFERING AND EVIL?

BY
GARRY POOLE
AND
JUDSON POLING

FOREWORD BY
LEE STROBEL

WILLOW CREEK
RESOURCES

ZondervanPublishingHouse
*Grand Rapids, Michigan*

*A Division of HarperCollinsPublishers*

*How Could God Allow Suffering and Evil?*
Copyright © 1998 by the Willow Creek Association

Requests for information should be addressed to:

📖 ZondervanPublishingHouse
*Grand Rapids, Michigan 49530*

ISBN: 0-310-22227-3

*Interior design by Sue Koppenol*

*Interior photography by Studio 139*

*Printed in the United States of America*

98 99 00 01 02 03 04 05 /❖EP / 10 9 8 7 6 5 4 3 2 1

# Contents

95414

# Foreword

For most of my life, I was an atheist. I thought that the Bible was hopelessly riddled with mythology, that God was a man-made creation born out of wishful thinking, and that the deity of Jesus was merely a product of legendary development. My no-nonsense education in journalism and law contributed to my skeptical viewpoint. In fact, just the idea of an all-powerful, all-loving, all-knowing creator of the universe seemed too absurd to even justify the time to investigate whether there could be any evidence backing it up.

However, my agnostic wife's conversion to Christianity and the subsequent transformation of her character and values prompted me to launch my own spiritual journey in 1980. Using the skills I developed as legal affairs editor of *The Chicago Tribune*, I began to check out whether any concrete facts, historical data, and convincing logic supported the Christian faith. Looking back, I wish I had this curriculum to supplement my efforts.

This excellent material can help you in two ways. If you're already a Christ follower, then this series can provide answers to some of the tough questions your seeker friends are asking—or that you're asking yourself. If you're not yet following Christ but consider yourself either an open-minded skeptic or a spiritual seeker, then this series can also help you in your journey. You can thoroughly and responsibly explore the relevant issues while discussing the topics in community with others. In short, it's a tremendous guide for people who really do want to find out the truth about God and this fascinating and challenging Nazarene carpenter named Jesus.

If the above paragraph in some way describes you, then prepare for the adventure of a lifetime. Let the pages that follow take you on a stimulating journey of discovery as you grapple with the most profound—and potentially life-changing—questions in the world.

—Lee Strobel
Author, *The Case for Christ:*
*A Journalist's Personal Investigation of the Evidence for Jesus*

# Tough Questions

The Tough Questions series was produced with the conviction that spiritual truth claims can and should be tested. Religious systems—sometimes considered exempt from scrutiny—are not free to make sweeping demands without providing reasons why they should be taken as fact. Religious truth, and Christianity in particular, purports to tell us about the most significant of life's mysteries, with consequences alleged to be *eternal*. This is a grand claim, and therefore should be analyzed carefully. If questioning shows weaknesses in such claims, it only makes sense to refuse to place trust in flawed systems of belief.

We contend God is not afraid of sincere questioning; in fact, it's a matter of historical record that Jesus wasn't. The Bible is not a secret kept only for the initiated few, but an open book, available for study and debate. The central teachings of Christianity are proclaimed to all, to the skeptic as well as to the seeker, like seeds cast freely in the wind.

Two things determine if those seeds will take hold in you and bring life: first, whether the seeds are alive (true), and second, whether they are allowed to germinate so their life can be experienced (implanted).

It is possible for any of us to believe error; it is also possible for us to resist truth. Using this set of discussion guides will help you sort out the true from the supposed, and offer a reasonable defense of the Christian faith. Whether you are a nonbeliever or skeptic, or someone who is already convinced and looking to fortify your faith, these guides will lead you to a fascinating exploration of vital truths.

## How to Use These Guides

These guides consist primarily of questions to be answered in a group setting. They elicit discussion rather than short, simple answers. Strictly speaking, these guides are not Bible studies, though they regularly refer to biblical themes and passages. They are topical discussion guides, meant to get you talking about what you really think and feel. The sessions have a point, and attempt to lead to some resolve, but they fall short of providing

the last word on any of the questions raised. You will be encouraged to bring your experience, perspectives, and uncertainties, and each group member will have to determine where he or she stands as the discussion progresses.

We have chosen a group format for exploring these questions primarily because we believe people learn best in active discussion rather than passive listening. It was not Jesus' preferred style to lecture, although He did do that. The amazing thing as we read the accounts of Jesus' life is how many times He stopped and asked people questions. Of course, He had a message to convey, but He knew listeners listen *best* when listened *to*. Dialogue awakens the mind. It honors each person, even if the person has inaccurate ideas. It shakes out the theories and beliefs that seem plausible when we've consulted only ourselves, and holds them up to the light of outside scrutiny. When this process has been followed, people see their own errors and more readily give up weak arguments in favor of better attested facts.

Your group should have a discussion leader. That facilitator can get needed background material in the *Tough Questions Leader's Guide*. It may very well happen, after some meetings, that group members are left with additional questions. This situation may be quite uncomfortable—people often prefer to tie up all loose ends before dismissing—but we hope the group will be open to letting the process of ongoing questioning lead to resolve. Try not to end every meeting with "Standard Answer #16" that doesn't really meet your need; instead, let the searching continue through the whole series (and beyond).

## Suggestions for Group Study

1. Read over the session before each meeting. Being familiar with the topic will greatly enrich your time in group discussion.
2. Be willing to join in the discussion. The leader of the group will not be lecturing but will encourage people to discuss their opinions. Plan to share honestly and forthrightly.
3. Stick to the topic being studied. You can't handle every tough question that comes to mind in one meeting.
4. Try to be sensitive to the other members of the group. Listen attentively when they speak, and be affirming whenever you can. This will encourage more hesitant members of the group to participate.

5. Be careful not to dominate the discussion. By all means participate, but allow others to have equal time.
6. It would be helpful to get a good modern translation of the Bible, such as the New International Version, the New American Standard Bible, or the New Revised Standard Version. We especially recommend *The Journey: A Bible for Seeking God and Understanding Life*, which has excellent notes for seekers. Questions in this guide are based on the New International Version.
7. Do some extra reading as you work through these sessions (see "For Further Reading" at the back of the guide).

## *Jesus Said What?*

Christianity is Christ, and Jesus left us with a boatload of hard sayings. The central scandal of Christianity is that God would come among us at a point in history in a person, Jesus of Nazareth. The most baffling moment of Jesus' life is the cross—that ignoble death, like a common criminal. In that place of weakness—where all seemed lost, where the taunts of "Prove yourself, Jesus, and come down from there!" lash like the whip that flogged Him prior to crucifixion—there, somehow, God was at His best, making His love more explicit than in a ten-thousand-page tome. That act of Jesus, presented as the ultimate defense of the love and justice of God, begs to be put to "cross"-examination.

We believe there are satisfying, reasonable answers to the hard questions about which we all wonder. We invite you to use these guides to explore them with a small group of fellow travelers. God bless you on your spiritual journey!

## *About This Series*

In 1992, Willow Creek Community Church, in partnership with Zondervan Publishing House and the Willow Creek Association, released a curriculum for small groups entitled the Walking with God series. In just three years, almost half a million copies of these small group study guides were being used in churches around the world. The phenomenal response to this curriculum affirmed the need for relevant and biblical small group materials.

7

At the writing of this curriculum, there are over 1,650 small groups meeting regularly within the structure of Willow Creek Community Church. That number continues to swell, including groups specifically designed to allow seekers a chance to raise questions and explore the basics of the faith. Many other churches throughout the world are growing in their commitment to small group ministries as well, so the need for resources is increasing.

In response to this demand, the Tough Questions small group series has been developed. Willow Creek Association and Zondervan Publishing House have joined together to create a fresh approach to providing materials like these for your groups. We hope you will benefit as you use these books to engage in lively discussion.

### Additional Resources and Teaching Materials

At the end of this study guide you will find some more information about the Willow Creek Resources® line. We hope you'll take advantage of those materials and events to further your spiritual progress.

# How Could God Allow Suffering and Evil?

Adolph Hitler. Tornadoes. Inoperable cancer. Car accidents. Terrorist bombings. AIDS. Drive-by shootings. Child abuse.

With just a few words, a chill runs down our spine, and we feel a sick tension in our stomach. Images flash before us that generate deep emotional reactions. What is it stirring up all our fear, outrage, and anger? It can be summed up in one word: *evil*.

When something terrible happens to us, we grope for explanations. Why does evil torment our lives? Where does it come from? How will we ever get past it?

Some people blame nature and its randomness. Some blame a few sinister but powerful people. Some blame themselves. Some believe there is a malicious force at work, a devil or evil spirits. And each of us—at one time or another—has probably blamed God.

Where does evil come from? Isn't it reasonable—maybe even logically necessary—to ascribe it to God? He made everything; He must have also made evil. And what exactly is evil? Is it a living entity, aiming its terrifying arrows with malice at hapless humans? Is it mere randomness—chaos masquerading as unkindness? Or maybe evil is part of God—the "Dark Side of the Force" that's as necessary as His good side.

> *If any spirit created the universe, it is malevolent, not benevolent.*
> —Quentin Smith, *The Anthropic Coincidences, Evil and the Disconfirmation of Theism*

Maybe God's testing us. He's waiting to see how we'll handle all this pain and suffering. Maybe it's punishment—He's telling us, "This is what you deserve for the life you've lived!" Or maybe the universe just got away from God, like a science experiment gone awry. He'd like to fix it, but it's just too out of control.

All of these thoughts about evil can lead us to one nagging question: Why does God allow it? Maybe right now, this is *your*

big question. If it is, you're in the right place. We invite you to explore this issue in all its rawness, being honest with yourself and with others about the pain and confusion you feel.

Six sessions discussing this subject will probably not answer every question, and it certainly won't heal every ache in your heart. But Christianity does purport to deal with this issue, and the Bible speaks to the reasons behind evil and the way for us to cope with it. We invite you to tread carefully, but deliberately, and to see for yourself if there are not answers—and encouragement—awaiting.

# Where Did Evil Come From?

### What's Wrong with This Picture?

Look around us. We live in a messed-up world. Disease, death, and misery envelop the planet. Strife exists between people and nations. This is a dark place to live, and while at times a ray of beauty or hope shines through, it is snatched away by the next senseless murder or "natural" disaster. Is this the world God created? Surely the "perfect world" story of the Garden of Eden was a myth. This planet could have never existed in that condition. Suffering and evil are the unvarnished facts of "creation"—not that fairy tale of a paradise.

> *If such a God did exist, he could not be a beneficent God, such as the Christians posit. What effrontery is it that talks about the mercy and goodness of a nature in which all animals devour animals, in which every mouth is a slaughter-house and every stomach a tomb!*
> —E. M. McDonald, *An Anthology of Atheism and Rationalism*

In his novel *Catch–22*, one of Joseph Heller's characters, Yossarian, holds the following conversation with Lt. Scheisskopf's wife:

> "Don't tell me God works in mysterious ways. There's nothing so mysterious about it. He's not working at all. He's playing. Or else He's forgotten all about us.... How much reverence can you have for a Supreme being who finds it necessary to include such phenomena as phlegm and tooth decay in His divine system of creation? What in the world was going through that warped, evil, scatological mind of His when He robbed old people of the ability to control their bowel movements? Why in the world

11

did He ever create pain? ... Why couldn't He have used a doorbell instead to notify us, or one of His celestial choirs? Or a system of red-and-blue neon tubes right in the middle of each person's forehead? ... What a colossal, immortal blunderer! When you consider the opportunity and power He had to really do a job, and then look at the stupid, ugly little mess He made of it instead, His sheer incompetence is almost staggering. ...Why, no self-respecting businessman would hire a bungler like Him as even a shipping clerk!"

"Stop it! Stop it!" Lieutenant Scheisskopf's wife screamed suddenly. ... "Stop it!"

"I thought you didn't believe in God," he asked bewilderedly.

"I don't," she sobbed. ... "But the God I don't believe in is a good God, a just God, a merciful God. He's not the mean and stupid God you make him out to be."

In the face of the undeniable existence of pain and evil, who *can* believe in a good God behind this mess? We must conclude He's either a poor creator, or a poor redeemer. He either intended this mess—what a shudder goes through us at that thought—or once He made the mistake, He was too inept to make it right.

Is there any possible excuse for the way things are? If this is all from God, what explains the origin—and persistence—of that which is supposed to be antithetical to His nature?

> Do you think that, if you were granted omnipotence and omniscience and millions of years in which to perfect your world, you could produce nothing better than the Ku Klux Klan, the Fascists, and Mr. Winston Churchill?
> —Bertrand Russell, *Why I Am Not a Christian*

> The Bible tells us to be like God, and then on page after page it describes God as a mass murderer. This may be the single most important key to the political behavior of Western Civilization.
> —Robert A. Wilson, *Right Where You Are Sitting Now*

## *Open for Discussion*

**1.** Describe a recent encounter you've had with some form of evil which prompted you to wonder why this kind of thing ever happens.

**2.** Who or what did you blame for the wrong that occurred in the situation you described above? (Give reasons for your response.) How did those around you see the situation?

**STRAIGHT TALK** **MORAL AND NATURAL EVIL**

Philosophers have categorized two kinds of evil:

*Moral evil*—man's own inhumanity to man, based on hate, greed, or overindulgence

*Natural evil*—evils brought on by natural causes in the world such as floods, earthquakes, or tornadoes and different sorts of diseases, accidents, and injuries. (We will look more closely at natural evil in Session 3.)

**3.** Using your previous example, would you categorize that experience with evil as moral evil, natural evil, or a combination of the two? Why? Does the category or type of evil influence your determination of where you will place the blame for evil?

**4.** Give your best shot at briefly explaining why we live in a world filled with so much evil and suffering.

> *Either God wants to abolish evil, and cannot; or he can, but does not want to; or he cannot and does not want to. If he wants to, but cannot, he is impotent. If he can, but does not want to, he is wicked. But, if God both can and wants to abolish evil, then how comes evil in the world?*
> —Epicurus, 350-?270 B.C.

### STRAIGHT TALK  UNWILLING OR UNABLE?

Doesn't it make sense that God, by default, is the author of evil if He created everything else? This progression of thought usually brings people full circle back to wondering what kind of God exists—or even if He exists.

Echoing Epicurus, David Hume, the eighteenth-century Scottish skeptic, put it this way, "Is He willing to prevent evil, but not able? Then He is impotent. Is He able, but not willing? Then He is malevolent. Is He both able and willing? Whence then is evil?"

**5.** Summarized below are two conclusions based on the above observations. Defend or refute the logic behind each:

Because we live in a world where evil does exists:

- God must not really exist after all; otherwise, He would not have created such a place filled with evil.
- God might still exist, but not in the way the Bible depicts Him (as all-powerful and loving); otherwise, He would have had both the ability and desire to create a world without so much evil.

### FREE CHOICE

Here is a very different argument addressing the problem of evil:

1. God created the universe without evil and suffering.
2. God created humans perfect.
3. God created humans with a perfect ability to freely choose between staying in harmony with God or rejecting Him.
4. Mankind freely chose to turn away from God.
5. Evil and suffering entered the world as a result of that separation from God.

Norman Geisler states it this way: "We have a real choice about what we do. God made us that way so we could be like Him and could love freely (forced love is not love at all, is it?). But in making us that way, He also allowed for the possibility of evil. To be free we had to have not only the opportunity to choose good, but also the ability to choose evil. That was the risk God knowingly took. That doesn't make Him responsible for evil. He created the *fact* of freedom; we perform the *acts* of freedom. He (God) made evil *possible;* men made evil *actual.*"

And Cliffe Knechtle states in his book *Give Me an Answer*: "Genesis 1 clearly communicates that when God created, all his creation was very good. God did not create evil, suffering or death. He created us to enjoy himself, each other and to celebrate his gift of life. Genesis 3 is the tragic record of how man and woman chose to reject God. The Bible, history books and the morning newspaper record how an immeasurable amount of evil has followed in the wake of human rebellion against God. The vast majority of this carnage is a direct result of human choice."

**6.** The above explanation introduces the element of a free choice by mankind to reject or accept God—with resulting consequences. Given the magnitude of the risk, what value do you suppose God placed on granting people freedom of choice (according to this perspective)?

*Babies are born with multiple birth defects. Genetic disorders plague many of us. An earthquake levels a city, and thousands lose their lives in the rubble. The Bible teaches that there is not always a one-to-one correspondence between sin and suffering. When we human beings told God to shove off, he partially honored our request. Nature began to revolt. The earth was cursed. Genetic breakdown and disease began. Pain and death became a part of the human experience. The Good creation was marred. We live in an unjust world. We are born into a world made chaotic and unfair by a humanity in revolt against its Creator.*

—Cliffe Knechtle, *Give Me an Answer*

**7.** How do you explain the correlation between being separated from God and the entrance of evil and suffering in the world?

*Freedom is not in unlimited options, but an unfettered choice between whatever options there are. As long as the choosing comes from the individual rather than an outside force, the decision is made freely. Free will means the ability to make an unforced decision between two or more options.*

—Norman Geisler and Ron Brooks, *When Skeptics Ask*

**8.** Share your opinion of the following statement:
God cannot create humans with free will (allowing for meaningful choices) and at the same time control them so they always choose good.

**9.** Do you consider your freedom to choose as a gift from God? Why or why not?

**10.** If you had the chance to give away your free will, but in so doing would never sin again, would you do it? Explain.

**11.** What do you do when you find yourself becoming angry at God for the things that go wrong in your life?

### PERSONAL PROFILE

### HOW COULD GOD LET THIS HAPPEN?

Joan had everything a woman could want: a loving husband, two healthy young children, a college education, a beautiful home, and on top of that was involved in a wonderful church. Yet her life was plagued by a dark cloud. Her father had been abusive—he had spent time in prison for attempting to murder her mother—and he had also sexually abused Joan when she was a little girl. More and more, Joan began to realize she had never really dealt with the pain and dysfunction from her childhood. Sadly, once she decided to look at these facts squarely, she got emotionally worse—not better. Deep depression set in, and she had to be hospitalized on more than one occasion.

At one of her points of intense despair, she asked her therapist, "Where was God during all this? Why didn't He step in and stop the abuse? I was just a little girl—what power did I have? How could He have let this happen to me?"

**12.**  What would you have told Joan if you were her therapist?

## Charting Your Journey

With this session, you're beginning a journey. Keep in mind that you do not need to feel pressure to "say the right thing" at any point during these discussions. You're taking the time to do this work because you want answers and because you're willing to be honest with your doubts and uncertainties. You may also have others in your life who would benefit from hearing about what you'll be learning. So use these sessions profitably—ask the tough questions, think "outside the box," learn from what others in your group have to say. But keep being authentic about where you are in your process.

To help you see yourself more clearly, throughout this guide you will have an opportunity to indicate where you are in your spiritual journey. As you gain more information, you may find yourself reconsidering your opinions from week to week. The important thing is for you to be completely truthful about what you believe—or don't believe—right now.

Check the statement(s) below which best describes your position at this point. Give reasons for your response.

_____ I believe that the origin of evil is God's ultimate responsibility.

_____ I'm convinced that evil is the result of mankind's rejection of God.

_____ Evil is a misnomer; the universe operates without a moral component.

_____ I'm pretty sure that man's freedom to choose is a gift from God.

_____ I'm pretty sure that man's freedom to choose has nothing to do with God.

_____ I find myself blaming God for things that go wrong in my life.

_____ I find myself blaming myself for things that go wrong in my life.

_____ Other: _____

# Why Doesn't God Do Something?

### A Good Story Gone Bad?

The lead character in the spy novel you're reading is in a terrible fix. They've got him tied up and are planning to torch the cabin where he's hidden away. You lean forward in your chair as the action intensifies, wondering how he'll escape. The villains drench the foundation of the cabin in gasoline. With a single match a bright yellow blaze envelops the walls in seconds.

The hero is trapped. He calls for help. He tries to loosen the cords that cut into his wrists. He kicks against the chair and tries to bash it against the wall and break free, but nothing works. Soon, smoke billows into the room. He's overcome by the thick, dark clouds. He passes out. Within a few minutes, his barely breathing form is engulfed in flames, and the hero is gone.

What? Dead? That can't be! You look to the next chapter, thinking he will have escaped somehow. Or maybe the cabin sequence was a dream. But the hero is dead. The bad guys have won. Evil triumphed. You hurl the book across the room.

"It's not fair! Why didn't the author write a better ending? Why did the good guy lose? That's not the way it should end!" But the author didn't write it that way. He allowed the hero to die.

That's how real life seems much of the time. When a little boy dies of leukemia in spite of hundreds of prayers, it seems like the story isn't ending the right way. When the young woman with so much life ahead of her dies in a car accident, it's like somebody made a huge mistake. When the relationship ends, and you feel the crushing weight of failure, you wish someone would rewrite your life's story.

When Elie Wiesel was a prisoner in a Nazi concentration camp at Birkenbau, he describes how a young boy was tortured and then hanged. The prisoners were forced to file by the boy, witnessing up close the punishment meted out on those who dared resist. The man behind Wiesel whispered through tears of rage, "Where is God now!?" In that moment, Wiesel writes, "I heard a voice within me answer him, 'Where is He? Here He is—He is hanging here on this gallows.'" In the face of evil, God dies for many of us.

Is God out there, writing the script, or not? If God's in charge, why doesn't He get down here and write us a better ending?

> So how do theists respond to arguments like this? They say there is a reason for evil, but it is a mystery. Well, let me tell you this: I'm actually one hundred feet tall even though I only appear to be six feet tall. You ask me for proof of this. I have a simple answer: it's a mystery. Just accept my word for it on faith. And that's just the logic theists use in their discussions of evil.
>
> —Quentin Smith, *Two Ways to Defend Atheism*

## Open for Discussion

1.  Have you ever wished that God would step in and rewrite the ending to a story in your life or the life of someone close to you? Share an example.

> There is virtually nothing which the Christian will accept as evidence of God's evil. If disasters that are admittedly "unmerited, pointless, and incapable of being morally rationalized" (quoting Hick) are compatible with the "goodness" of God, what could possibly qualify as contrary evidence? The "goodness" of God, it seems, is compatible with any state of affairs. While we evaluate a man with reference to his actions, we are not similarly permitted to judge God. God is immune from the judgment of evil as a matter of principle.
>
> —George Smith, *Atheism: The Case Against God*

**2.** Habakkuk cries out to God, "Your eyes are too pure to look on evil; you cannot tolerate wrong. Why then do you tolerate the treacherous? Why are you silent while the wicked swallow up those more righteous than themselves?" (Habakkuk 1:13). How do you think God would answer the prophet Habakkuk's accusations against Him?

**3.** What does the fact that Habakkuk can even raise these issues with God tell you about God's openness to tough questions directed at Him?

**4.** Listed below are a set of scenarios describing how God could step in and solve the problem of evil and suffering. Select the one you like best and give some reasons for your selection. Which ones do you think are *not* good options?

- God could destroy us. He is supposedly all-powerful and perfectly capable of wiping out the human race. If there weren't any people, no one would hurt anyone, and no one would get hurt. Nature could spew volcanic blasts, rattle the earth with quakes, and flood the plains, and the only life-forms affected would be plants and animals.
- God could handpick the evil people and eliminate them. All murderers, rapists, despots—any truly wicked person—would go. Anyone who would eventually commit evil, even

if it hadn't happened yet, would also be terminated. The rest of us would be left to live in peace.

- God could step in and override every evil act. When someone shoots another person, the guy who gets shot just gets up, grins, and goes on with life, like a character in a cartoon. If you drive off a cliff, you are a bit dazed for a minute or two, but then you shake it off. Our choices would make no difference. People would be immortal, like Superman, unable to be hurt or die.

- God could choose to stay out of things and let us fend for ourselves. We would just do our best and make our own choices and let the pieces fall where they may. He would watch, totally dispassionate, totally uninvolved, totally unconnected with our existence.

- God could periodically step in, unbeknownst to us. God could actually make a difference in minimizing evil or eliminating it at times. But we would never know what He was up to, and we would never know to whom He was going to show mercy or who was just out of luck.

- God could get a taste of what we go through by experiencing the evil of the world personally and knowing what it feels like. We would then be able to see exactly how God would respond to the everyday frustrations and disappointments in facing evil and suffering firsthand.

*I contend that we are both atheists. I just believe in one fewer god than you do. When you understand why you dismiss all the other possible gods, you will understand why I dismiss yours.*

—Stephen Roberts

**5.** Suppose God did step in and wipe out every trace of evil. According to Romans 3:23, "*All* have sinned and fall short of the glory of God." What would that do to the human population? Where would that leave you?

**6.** If there were no sin in the world, do you think there would be any suffering and evil? Why or why not?

## *Heart of the Matter*

Cliffe Knechtle has the following to say about love and choice:

> I deeply love my wife, Sharon. Suppose all I had to do to hear her say "I love you, Cliffe" was to push a button in her back and out it would come. That wouldn't be love. That wouldn't be a relationship. It would be a programmed response from a computer. A relationship demands love. Love requires a choice. It cannot be forced. God created us in His image. That means when God commands, we can obey or disobey.

**7.** Given the above quote, would it have been better if God would have created us without an ability to choose evil in the first place? Why or why not?

**8.** 2 Peter 3:9 reads, "The Lord ... is patient with you, not wanting anyone to perish, but everyone to come to repentance." What insight does this verse give concerning one reason God currently tolerates evil?

**9.** What advantages are there to allowing people to see evil firsthand, and then having them reject it in favor of living under God's leadership? Do you believe this is the best way to deal with evil? Why or why not?

## GOD'S ULTIMATE PLAN FOR EVIL

Revelation 21:1, 3–5 describes God's ultimate plan for evil. In this passage, the apostle John sees a vision of the future:

Then I saw a new heaven and a new earth, for the first heaven and the first earth had passed away... And I heard a loud voice... saying, "Now the dwelling of God is with men, and he will live with them. They will be his people, and God himself will be with them and be their God. He will wipe every tear from their eyes. There will be no more death or mourning or crying or pain, for the old order of things has passed away." He who was seated on the throne said, "I am making everything new!"

**10.** If you knew for sure that God promises to rid the world of evil somehow, some way, in His own time, how would you feel about having to tolerate evil and suffering now? What problems would still remain for you?

## A GRAND FINALE

It seems that God allows evil so that men and women who are evil can have an opportunity to turn back to Him. If He stops evil, He also stops the process by which people can come to Him and prevents the possibility of winning their hearts. People would lose their chance of knowing God and living with Him for eternity.

God is just. He has a divine understanding of right and wrong. Not only can He hear each side's case, He also knows all the hidden motives and thoughts behind them. As a result, God promises justice, and we can be sure that when it comes it will be absolute and totally satisfying.

The story of God and man and evil isn't over. There's a grand finale yet to come, and it would be unfair to judge the "Author" without letting Him write the last chapter. The good news is, He already has the "rough draft" and it's in the Bible—we know how the story is going to end. Some of the details will become clear only in the future, but based on what God has shown us already, we can trust Him for a *great* ending.

In his book *Give Me an Answer*, Cliffe Knechtle recounts the following story:

> During World War II the guards at a Japanese prisoner-of-war camp would take the English soldiers out into the fields to do hard manual labor. At the end of one day the guards lined up the English prisoners and counted the tools. They found that one shovel was missing. A guard called out, "Who stole the shovel?" No one responded. The Japanese guard cocked his rifle and said, "All die! All die!"
>
> Suddenly one Scottish soldier stepped forward and said, "I stole the shovel." Instantly he was shot dead. His comrades gathered up his body and the remaining tools and went back to the prisoner-of-war compound. Back in the prison camp, the Japanese guards counted the tools again. They found that no shovel was missing. The Scottish soldier had sacrificed his life that his buddies might live.
>
> Two thousand years ago God became man. His name was Jesus Christ. He lived a perfect life. He never did anything wrong. He did not deserve to die. He stepped forward and bled and died on a cross to pay the penalty that you and I deserve for having stolen, cheated, lied, dishonored our parents and ignored God. Your guilt and my guilt point to the wrong we have done. The cross of Jesus Christ points to the depth of God's love for us. You and I must decide to ask Christ for forgiveness and to commit our lives to him.

Referring to the story of Elie Wiesel in the concentration camp (found in the Introduction to this session), Philip Yancey observes, "The voice within Wiesel [which said God was hanging dead just like that boy] spoke truth: in a way, God did hang [there]....God did not exempt even himself from human suffering. He too hung on a gallows, at Calvary, and that alone is what keeps me believing in a God of love."

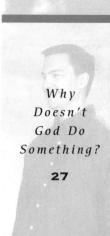

**11.** What is your reaction to the claim that Jesus Christ, out of His great love for you, died on your behalf to pay the penalty for the evil in *your* life?

**12.** If Jesus Christ and His death for you were all God gave you to help you cope with evil in your life, would that be enough? What else would you need?

### GOD, A WIMP?

**PERSONAL PROFILE**

Joan, who had been sexually abused as a child, began to question everything she believed about God. Although she'd become a committed Christian years before, she had serious doubts about the goodness of God, and now had trouble trusting Him.

For many years, she had had dreams that some day in the future she would be raped, and that she would then tell others how she got through it. In her dreams, God allowed her to be raped so He could, in her words, "Get lots of glory for how He healed me emotionally." Now, she realized her reoccurring dream held a dark truth: the rape she feared *might* happen, *had* happened. It was as if, at an unconscious level, she was trying to reckon with how horrible it was to have God as the source of her suffering.

Once, a friend tried to console her. "You know, Joan, God was right there with you when all this happened. He saw it all and wept with you."

"That's just great!" she replied. "Then God is a wimp who stood there in the corner of the room and watched it all. I can just see Him, hands in His pockets, watching me cry out for help as a little girl and doing nothing. What human parent in His right mind would stand idly by? Is that all the better God's help gets?"

**13.** What is your reaction to Joan's friend's words? What do you think about Joan's response?

## Charting Your Journey

Check the statement(s) below which best describes your position at this point. Give reasons for your response.

_____ It makes no sense that God would allow evil in this world.

_____ It's impossible to really know why God does not do more to stop all this evil and suffering.

_____ I'm glad God has not wiped out all evil yet—otherwise I'd be gone too.

_____ If God really loved us, He would not let us suffer so much.

_____ The benefits of God allowing us to make free-will choices far outweighs any costs.

_____ Other:_____

*Why Doesn't God Do Something?*

# Why Do Innocent People Suffer?

### It's Not Fair

The man in the interview struggled to stay in control. He clutched the shoulders of his wife, who grieved openly. The reporter was speaking to the couple in front of their little boy's school. Nearby lay a toppled bike. Blood covered the sidewalk.

"Two nine-year-old boys had just left school on their bikes when shots rang out from a passing car," the reporter stated, facing the cameras. "One boy was hit, and died on the way to the hospital. Police are searching for any clues that could explain the motives in this senseless shooting, or lead to the capture of the murderer."

"Why? Why my baby boy?" the broken man pleaded. "He didn't do anything to anyone! He was just riding his bike!"

The parents wept, and neighbors wrapped their arms around the couple to console them. The camera cut away to a school picture of a fresh-faced boy, grinning, a few teeth missing, happy and apparently carefree. Innocence personified. Innocence lost.

Why do the innocent suffer?

Some of the most shocking images from the Holocaust are those of the children, elderly, and simple-minded who were victims of that injustice. Their bodies shriveled, yet living . . . if it could be called living. Working in the camps. Hiding. Dying. These helpless ones needed care, not mistreatment, shelter and protection, not punishment. They harmed no one and deserved to live full lives and die in dignity. But they didn't get that chance.

Why do the innocent suffer?

Native Americans, a proud but now subdued people, were driven from their homes by "newcomers" who claimed the land as their own, and were forced to march along what would come to be known as the Trail of Tears. Women and children stumbled, weeping, shivering in the frigid winter snows. Many died along the way. Decades earlier, these same "newcomers" had raided another continent, carrying away its citizens to become slaves of their growing nation. Ironically, many of these "newcomers" believed they were allowed by God to engage in such barbarism.

Why do the innocent suffer?

How can God sit by and let evil affect the innocent, the gentle, the helpless souls who mean no harm to anyone? It's a fair question, put to a God who claims He represents all that is just: Why do the innocent suffer?

> If a plane crashes and 99 people die while 1 survives, it is called a miracle. Should the families of the 99 think so?
> —Judith Hayes, *In God We Trust: But Which One?*

### *Open for Discussion*

**1.** Share a personal example of a time when you or someone close to you experienced suffering for no just reason.

**2.** Do you agree with the following passage, which teaches that evil people flourish and the innocent suffer? Give examples to support your answer.

> For I envied the arrogant when I saw the prosperity of the wicked. They have no struggles; their bodies are healthy and strong. They are free from the burdens common to man; they are not plagued by human ills. . . . This is what the wicked are like—always carefree, they increase in wealth. Surely in vain have I kept my heart pure; in vain have I washed my hands in innocence. All day long I have been plagued; I have been punished every morning (Psalm 73:3–5, 12–14).

**3.** All suffering is the result of either an act of nature, an act (or lack thereof) of one or more people (human or demonic), or a poor choice by the suffering individual. Many times it may be a combination of these sources. Which source(s) produced the suffering you described in question one? Based on these categories, where do your feelings of blame or anger get directed? Explain.

**4.** When tornadoes, earthquakes, floods, disease, and other acts of nature cause tremendous suffering in the lives of people, which of the explanations listed below seem reasonable to you? Why?

- God is in control, and He orchestrates these hardships as a way to punish people or teach them lessons.
- God has given up control, therefore, everything that happens does so on the basis of chance.

> Not long ago I was sleeping in a cabin in the woods and was awoken in the middle of the night by the sounds of a struggle between two animals. Cries of terror and extreme agony rent the night, intermingled with the sounds of jaws snapping bones and flesh being torn from limbs. One animal was being savagely attacked, killed and then devoured by another. A clearer case of a horrible event in nature, a natural evil, has never been presented to me. It seemed to me self-evident that the natural law that animals must savagely kill and devour each other in order to survive was an evil natural law and that the obtaining of this law was sufficient evidence that God did not exist.
> —Quentin Smith, An Atheological Argument from Evil Natural Laws

- God is in control but still allows these things—both good and bad—to happen.
- Acts of nature causing harm are really acts of the devil not God.
- All suffering caused by nature is the direct result of sin entering the world which created chaos within the system.
- No one knows the answer to such a difficult question—it's pointless to speculate.

> *Believing God is the sovereign creator and in control of the world doesn't mean He is directly, causally connected with everything that happens on this earth. He doesn't make the decision to reach down and shake loose a rock to start every avalanche.*
>
> *When some people hear this kind of thinking, they get nervous. They think I'm limiting God. I'm not. But I am saying God doesn't ordinarily interfere with the natural course of the universe any more often than He directly interferes with man's choices.*
>
> —Jay Kesler, *Making Life Make Sense*

**5.** If God isn't directly controlling everything that happens, what's a reasonable explanation of natural disasters?

> *The vast majority of human evil and suffering is a direct result of human irresponsibility.*
> —Cliffe Knechtle, *Give Me an Answer*

**6.** Describe a time when you in some way deserved the suffering you were experiencing. Did you still have the tendency to want to blame someone or something outside yourself? Why?

**7.** What do you think of the following statement: When someone contracts a disease that is a direct result of a lifestyle choice (such as a drug-user contracting AIDS or a lifelong cigarette smoker who gets lung cancer) the responsibility for that suffering must lie squarely on the shoulders of the person who made that choice. We, as outsiders, have no obligation to offer compassion.

**8.** In light of the pain we bring upon ourselves, what conclusions can you make about the logic behind God's guidelines and warnings in the Bible such as, "Hate what is evil; cling to what is good" (Romans 12:9)?

> He [the Father in heaven] causes his sun to rise on the evil and the good, and sends rain on the righteous and the unrighteous.
> —Matthew 5:45

**9.** What point is C. S. Lewis trying to get across when he states, "The question is not 'Why do the innocent suffer?' but rather 'Why don't we all suffer more?'" Do you agree with him? Why or why not?

## Heart of the Matter

Suffering is hard. And it can hurt at such a deep level. As we endure personal pain and suffering in our lives, we may often use phrases such as "Why is this happening to me?" or "This isn't fair." But suffering is more than an intellectual problem. We are probably more intent on finding help and relief than answers, and we certainly don't want someone giving us what they feel is the "right answer" in an unfeeling way.

The Bible recognizes the need to go beyond explaining pain to a sufferer, and so encourages us to "weep with those who weep." It is a practice Jesus Himself modeled. People going through dark valleys are looking for compassion, not just pat answers from someone more concerned with being correct than with showing concern.

**10.** Can you think of any positive things that come out of our suffering? Share a personal example, if you have one.

> We also rejoice in our sufferings, because we know that suffering produces perseverance; perseverance, character; and character, hope.
>
> Romans 5:3–4

> God whispers to us in our pleasures, speaks in our conscience, but shouts in our pains: it is His megaphone to rouse a deaf world.
>
> —C. S. Lewis

**11.** Has God ever used pain and suffering in your life to get your attention? What was He wanting to get across to you?

**12.** What do you think are some possible alternatives to pain and suffering that God could have used to capture your attention?

*You see, Jesus endured a suffering beyond all comprehension: He bore the punishment for the sins of the whole world. None of us can comprehend that suffering. Though He was innocent, He voluntarily underwent the punishment for your sins and mine. And why? Because He loves you so much. How can you reject Him who gave up everything for you.*

—William Lane Craig, *No Easy Answer*

**SESSION**
**THREE**

**36**

### A WORD FROM GOD

As we encounter hard times, God offers words of encouragement and comfort. A few examples from the Bible are listed here:

He who did not spare his own Son, but gave him up for us all—how will he not also, along with him, graciously give us all things?... Who shall separate us from the love of Christ? Shall trouble or hardship or persecution or famine or nakedness or danger or sword?... No, in all these things we are more than conquerors through him who loved us. For I am convinced that neither death nor life, neither angels nor demons, neither the present nor the future, nor any powers, neither height nor depth, nor anything else in all creation, will be able to separate us from the love of God that is in Christ Jesus our Lord (Romans 8:32, 35, 37–39).

So then, those who suffer according to God's will should commit themselves to their faithful Creator and continue to do good (1 Peter 4:19).

I consider that our present sufferings are not worth comparing with the glory that will be revealed in us (Romans 8:18).

And we know that in all things God works for the good of those who love him, who have been called according to his purpose (Romans 8:28).

**13.** People who refuse to let God work in their lives have no promises in the Bible about any benefits from suffering. However, the above verses assure those who *do* allow God to rule in their lives that something good can come from hard times. In what ways can the truth of these verses bring comfort in the suffering you endure?

### GOD, A WISE FRIEND

Joan continued in her struggle to comprehend what had happened to her as a child, and to try to make some sense of it.

At first, when well-meaning friends tried to console her by telling her God was with her, she was angry. In her view, God had been a powerless spectator, standing in the corner with His hands in His pockets, letting the rape continue.

But as time went on, she began to see His role differently. She realized that He had not been over in a corner, but right there beside her, kneeling down, stroking her hair and whispering in her ear words of comfort. He was telling her that there would come a time when she would be older and surrounded by people who would help her, and at that time she could take these experiences out of her subconscious and process them. By giving her a strong mind that could endure the rape, God had made sure she would make it to a safe place later, where she could go beyond the hurt to true healing.

**14.** What is your reaction to Joan's changing view of God? In your opinion, is it enough that God enabled her to survive and get help later? Explain.

## *Charting Your Journey*

Check the statement(s) below which best describes your position at this point. Give reasons for your response.

_____ I still cannot understand why God would allow innocent people to suffer.

_____ I can understand that suffering could be used as an "attention-getter," but I think a loving God would think of a better way to make that happen.

_____ The benefits for God allowing people to make choices must far outweigh the costs.

_____ The suffering I have experienced in my own life has driven me away from God.

_____ It is good to know suffering is only temporary.

_____ I don't understand it all, but I trust the way God is handling suffering in my life and in this world.

_____ Other: _____

# Is the Devil for Real?

### A Harmless Mask?

Mary winds her cart down the crowded aisles of the local Wal-Mart, shoving a handful of raisins at her wailing eighteen-month-old strapped in the front of the cart.

"Hurry up, Tucker," she calls to her lagging six-year-old son as they arrive at the aisle marked "Halloween costumes."

"There it is!" the boy exclaims as he races down the aisle, jumping over witches wigs and green face paint that have been carelessly knocked to the floor. He snatches his choice off the rack and runs back to his weary mother, who is wiping off his baby sister's nose.

"Here!" He shoves the costume in the cart. Mary looks down to see a plastic pitchfork and a red cape and horns coated with red glitter. Stapled to it is a plastic bag with the words "devil make-up included." Mary picks up the costume. "Let's see what else we can find . . . maybe a nice cowboy outfit," she says firmly to her son as she reaches to hang the devil outfit back on the rack.

"Mary?"

Mary turns to see Beth, her friend from the carpool. "Hi, Beth!"

"You look good in red," Beth says with a laugh.

Mary shakes her head. "I just can't bring myself to let Tucker run around in this thing. It's seems so . . . so, well, evil."

"Oh, what's the harm?" Beth shakes her head. "It's all just make-believe."

Mary quickly glances around at the shelves jammed with alternatives. She shrugs. "Yeah, I guess you're right. I mean, it's not like the devil is real." She sighs as she tosses the devil outfit back into her cart.

He's called "Satan," "the devil," "the Dragon," and "the Serpent." Whether we picture him as a goofy guy in red tights with horns or as a dark, evil creature lurking about in a long, black cape, most of us have an image of Satan. But most of us have dismissed that creature as a carryover from more superstitious times. Surely, in our scientific age, no one takes a personal, malevolent spiritual being seriously!

Is the devil real? Should he be feared? Or is he just a symbol, a myth, a personification of impersonal forces? This session will allow you to consider the reasons why we should take the matter of the devil seriously and explore what the Bible has to say about this fallen angel called Satan.

> *I do not pretend to be able to prove that there is no God. I equally cannot prove that Satan is a fiction. The Christian god may exist; so may the gods of Olympus, or of ancient Egypt, or of Babylon. But no one of these hypotheses is more probable than any other: they lie outside the region of even probable knowledge, and therefore there is no reason to consider any of them.*
>
> —Bertrand Russell

## Open for Discussion

**1.** Growing up, what did you believe about the devil? What most influenced your thinking?

> *I was not content to believe in a personal devil and serve him, in the ordinary sense of the word. I wanted to get hold of him personally and become his chief of staff.*
> —Aleister Crowley (1875–1947), British occultist

**2.** Do you currently believe an evil spiritual being exists? Why or why not? What is the value of trying to find out if such a being exists?

*We may not pay Satan reverence, for that would be indiscreet, but we can at least respect his talents. A person who has for untold centuries maintained the imposing position of spiritual head of four-fifths of the human race, and political head of the whole of it, must be granted the possession of executive abilities of the loftiest order.*

—Mark Twain

### SYMBOLIC OR REAL?

The search for the devil is not the search to prove there's evil in the universe; there is plenty of depravity bound up in the actions of people without having to refer to some other spiritual force at work to explain it. Yet the Bible says evil extends beyond humans. No less an authority than Jesus himself believed in the existence of this fallen angelic being, and He warned others to take the devil seriously.

**3.** What difference does it make to you that Jesus believed in the devil? What other evidence for the devil's existence (besides Jesus' acknowledgment of him) could be put forward?

### THE TEMPTATION IN THE WILDERNESS

The passage below tells of Jesus' encounter with the devil just before Jesus started His public ministry.

Then Jesus was led by the Spirit into the desert to be tempted by the devil. After fasting forty days and forty nights, he was hungry. The tempter came to him and said, "If you are the Son of God, tell these stones to become bread."

Jesus answered, "It is written: 'Man does not live on bread alone, but on every word that comes from the mouth of God.'"

Then the devil took him to the holy city and had him stand on the highest point of the temple. "If you are the Son of God," he said, "throw yourself down. For it is written: 'He will command his angels concerning you, and they will lift you up in their hands, so that you will not strike your foot against a stone.'"

Jesus answered him, "It is also written: 'Do not put the Lord your God to the test.'"

Again, the devil took him to a very high mountain and showed him all the kingdoms of the world and their splendor. "All this I will give you," he said, "if you will bow down and worship me."

Jesus said to him, "Away from me, Satan! For it is written: 'Worship the Lord your God, and serve him only.'"

Then the devil left him, and angels came and attended him (Matthew 4:1–11).

**4.** What did the devil seem to want from Jesus and what tactics did he employ? How did Jesus get the devil to leave Him alone?

**5.** The devil first shows up in the Bible in the Garden of Eden. What is the essence of his activity as described in the following passage?

Now the serpent was more crafty than any of the wild animals the LORD God had made. He said to the woman, "Did God really say, 'You must not eat from any tree in the garden'?" The woman said to the serpent, "We may eat fruit from the trees in the garden, but God did say, 'You must not eat fruit from the tree that is in the middle of the garden, and you must not touch it, or you will die.'" "You will not surely die," the serpent said to the woman. "For God knows that when you eat of it your eyes will be opened, and you will be like God . . ." (Genesis 3:1–5).

**6.** 1 Peter 5:8 says, "Your enemy the devil prowls around like a roaring lion looking for someone to devour." If the devil is an intelligent but rebellious angel, what do you think are his motives in trying to trip up and gain additional "God-rejecters" among humans?

**7.**  In the earlier chapters of the book of Job, we find that Satan is allowed (within limits) to afflict Job through natural calamities and physical ailments. What role might Satan play in the evil and suffering experienced in this world today?

**8.** Why do you suppose God doesn't just eliminate Satan now?

**9.** According to the verses below, what is the extent of the devil's power? What do you think about the fairness of this situation?

We know that we are children of God, and that the whole world is under the control of the evil one (1 John 5:19).

The god of this age has blinded the minds of unbelievers, so that they cannot see the light of the gospel of the glory of Christ . . . (2 Corinthians 4:4).

For our struggle is not against flesh and blood, but against the rulers, against the authorities, against the powers of this dark world and against the spiritual forces of evil in the heavenly realms (Ephesians 6:12).

### *Heart of the Matter*

**10.** What is your emotional response to the possibility of the devil's existence? What would help you determine, one way or the other, what the truth is concerning the devil?

**11.** Put into your own words the meaning behind what the Bible recommends in the following passages as defense against the devil:

Finally, be strong in the Lord and in his mighty power. Put on the full armor of God so that you can take your stand against the devil's schemes (Ephesians 6:10–11).

Submit yourselves, then, to God. Resist the devil, and he will flee from you (James 4:7).

And God is faithful; he will not let you be tempted beyond what you can bear (1 Corinthians 10:13).

## Charting Your Journey

Check the statement(s) below which best describes your position at this point. Give reasons for your response.

_____ I still have no confidence that Satan exists.

_____ Satan may exist, but I don't think he plays an active role in my life or the world around me.

_____ If God is all-powerful, I don't understand why He doesn't get rid of Satan now.

_____ This session left me with more questions than it answered.

_____ I believe Satan exists, and that frightens me.

_____ I believe Satan exists and is active in the world, but I am also confident that God is in control.

_____ I worry about the power Satan has to mess with my life.

_____ It bothers me that God has allowed Satan to have as much control as he has.

_____ Other: _____

*Is the Devil for Real?*

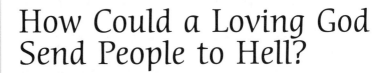
# How Could a Loving God Send People to Hell?

### A Good Man

Richard's a decent fellow. At age sixty-eight, he's raised his family, paid his mortgage, celebrated the birth of five grandkids, and retired to a comfortable home in the country. He never did anything bad—unlike some people with whom he had worked over the years. He never killed anyone, never pocketed company funds, never had an affair. He's just lived life. He hasn't bothered anyone, and everyone who knows him likes him.

Is this a man headed for hell?

> Life can be beautiful, profound, and awe-inspiring, even without an irate god threatening us with eternal torment.
> —Judith Hayes, *In God We Trust: But Which One?*

"I figure, at the end of my life," Richard says, "if there's a God, He'll look at me and say, 'Now here's an average guy if I ever saw one. As long as you didn't do anything too terrible, come on in.'

"Frankly, I don't see how a loving God could send *anyone* to hell—let alone a regular guy like me," Richard concludes.

Like Richard, many of us are counting on a points system of salvation, trusting that our good deeds will outweigh our bad. As long as God grades on a curve, most of us don't have a thing to worry about.

But what if the points don't add up in our favor? What if unkind intentions, selfish attitudes, lustful desires, and unseen motives factor in—all the things we thought were undetected? Worse, what if it's not enough just to tip the scales slightly in the direction of good? What if the presence of *any* sin is a problem?

**46**

But then again, some of us are hoping that God will just let all of us into heaven anyway.

"I've always heard God is love," Richard says. "Real love doesn't set up strict requirements for receiving it. It's unconditional. Certainly, limiting heaven only to people who follow Jesus is ridiculous. The whole idea of hell seems contrary to love."

> *I can hardly see how anyone ought to wish Christianity to be true: for if so the plain language of the text seems to show that the men who do not believe—and this would include my father, brother, and almost all of my best friends—will be everlastingly punished. And this is a damnable doctrine.*
> —Charles Darwin

Is Richard right? Will God give in and invite everyone into heaven after all?

Maybe there is no hell. Of course, it's a gamble to live as if hell didn't exist, because if we're wrong the result could be disastrous. But then again, even if there is a hell, if we're there with most of our friends, it might not be that bad.

There is one (pardon the pun) *surefire* way to find out. But do we really want to wait until it's too late to be certain? Can't we find any reliable information right now about the afterlife? So much is at stake. Even if there's only a five percent chance hell exists, shouldn't we try to gain a reasonable certainty about where we're headed?

> *Go to heaven for the climate, hell for the company.*
> —Mark Twain

> *God says, "do what you wish, but make the wrong choice and you will be tortured for eternity in hell." That ... would be akin to a man telling his girlfriend, do what you wish, but if you choose to leave me, I will track you down and blow your brains out. When a man says this we call him a psychopath and cry out for his imprisonment/execution. When God says the same we call him "loving" and build churches in his honor.*
> —William C. Easttom II

## Open for Discussion

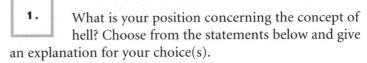

**1.** What is your position concerning the concept of hell? Choose from the statements below and give an explanation for your choice(s).

- No such place actually exists.
- It's just a figurative idea without any reality attached to it.
- It doesn't really matter, because there's no such thing as an afterlife.
- It's total separation from God forever.
- Hell is present in the here and now.
- It's a fun place to party all the time.
- People spend some time there and get to go to heaven later on.
- Only the really, really wicked will go to hell.
- It doesn't really matter, because all people will go to heaven anyway.

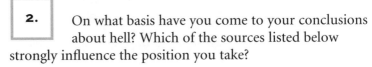

**2.** On what basis have you come to your conclusions about hell? Which of the sources listed below strongly influence the position you take?

- spiritual books
- spiritual leaders
- popular opinion
- common sense
- the Bible
- religious upbringing
- hopeful thinking
- personal experience

> *What is the function that a clergyman performs in the world? Answer: he gets his living by assuring idiots that he can save them from an imaginary hell.*
> —H. L. Mencken

| **3.** |
|---|

On a scale from 1 to 10 (1 being a weak level of reliability and 10 being a very strong level of reliability), how dependable are your sources of authority for your understanding about the idea of a hell?

 **SOME SAY YES, SOME SAY NO**

Opinions about the reality of hell—and the degree of certainty regarding those opinions—range widely. Consider the following few examples:

Do not be afraid of those who kill the body but cannot kill the soul. Rather, be afraid of the One who can destroy both soul and body in hell (Matthew 10:28).

The Lord Jesus, the Son of God, incarnate love himself, spoke more about the reality of hell and everlasting punishment for unbelievers than anyone else. Repeatedly, again and again in the discourses of Jesus, he warned his auditors, he pleaded with them to repent lest they perish (David L. Larsen).

Now, if anything at all can be known to be wrong, it seems to me to be unshakably certain that it would be wrong to make any sentient being suffer eternally for any offense whatever (Antony Flew, *God, Freedom, and Immortality*).

To rule by fettering the mind through fear of punishment in another world is just as base as to use force (Hypatia, Alexandrian mathematician, 415 A.D.).

| **4.** |
|---|

On what basis do the above people believe or not believe an actual place called hell exists? How does the reliability of their sources compare with yours?

## STRAIGHT TALK — HELL'S ENTRANCE WARNINGS

The Bible has several things to say about hell:

Enter through the narrow gate. For wide is the gate and broad is the road that leads to destruction, and many enter through it. But small is the gate and narrow the road that leads to life, and only a few find it (Matthew 7:13–14).

If anyone's name was not found written in the book of life, he was thrown into the lake of fire (Revelation 20:15).

But the cowardly, the unbelieving, the vile, the murderers, the sexually immoral, those who practice magic arts, the idolaters and all liars—their place will be in the fiery lake of burning sulfur. This is the second death (Revelation 21:8).

"The Son of Man will send out his angels, and they will weed out of his kingdom everything that causes sin and all who do evil. They will throw them into the fiery furnace, where there will be weeping and gnashing of teeth" (Matthew 13:41–42; see also Luke 16:19–31).

"Not everyone who says to me, 'Lord, Lord,' will enter the kingdom of heaven, but only he who does the will of my Father who is in heaven. Many will say to me on that day, 'Lord, Lord, did we not prophesy in your name, and in your name drive out demons and perform many miracles?' Then I will tell them plainly, 'I never knew you . . .'" (Matthew 7:21–23).

"O Jerusalem, Jerusalem, you who kill the prophets and stone those sent to you, how often I have longed to gather your children together, as a hen gathers her chicks under her wings, but you were not willing" (Matthew 23:37).

**5.** Based on the above verses, what are some of the reasons the Bible gives for why people end up in hell?

**6.** Based on the above verses, what observations can you make about what hell is really like?

> [The Bible] goes on about the wailing and gnashing of teeth. It comes in one verse after another, and it is quite manifest to the reader that there is a certain pleasure in contemplating the wailing and gnashing of teeth, or else it would not occur so often.
> —Bertrand Russell

> "Abandon hope all ye that enter here."
> —The inscription above entrance to hell in Dante's *Inferno*

**7.** What do you think of the following objections to the idea of hell. Can you come up with some of your own?

- If God is just, sending people to hell would be unfair.
- If God is love, hell would not be a result of love.
- Hell as a punishment for sin doesn't fit the crime.
- "Good" people—though admittedly not perfect—ought to be rewarded for their goodness.

## GOD'S VIEW OF HELL

**STRAIGHT TALK** Ultimately, God doesn't send anyone to hell; people *choose* to go there. People reject God in a variety of ways, and then spend an eternity living with the very choices they've made while here on earth. If they invited God to be with them, to be involved in their lives, to lead and direct them, to be Lord over all their decisions, then heaven is the place where that continues, only more so. If, on the other hand, people avoid God, find His laws restrictive and objectionable, prefer He not interfere in their plans, and reject His overtures of reconciliation, then hell is the place where that way of living is allowed forever. As C. S. Lewis pointed out, there are two kinds of people in the world: those who say to God, "Your will be done" and those to whom God says, "Your will be done."

The Bible emphasizes God's attitude toward people heading for hell:

"As surely as I live," declares the Sovereign LORD, "I take no pleasure in the death of the wicked, but rather that they turn from their ways and live. Turn! Turn from your evil ways! Why will you die, O house of Israel?" (Ezekiel 33:11).

He is patient with you, not wanting anyone to perish, but everyone to come to repentance (2 Peter 3:9).

**8.** What is your reaction to the above assertions? Which ideas do you agree with, and which ones do you disagree with? What conclusions can be drawn about God's desire concerning everyone's eternal destiny?

---

*We must picture Hell as a state where everyone is perpetually concerned about his own dignity and advancement, where everyone has a grievance, and where everyone lives the deadly serious passions of envy, self-importance, and resentment.*

—C. S. Lewis

## Heart of the Matter

How
Could a
Loving
God Send
People
to Hell?

53

**9.** Hell can be described as the place where God finally confines sin and evil—where He puts boundaries around it once and for all so it doesn't pollute the rest of the universe. How do you feel about the hope that evil will not have free reign forever?

> *If every Christian could spend one minute in the fires of hell, he would become a soul winner the rest of his life and to seek to warn men and women of the terrible and tragic fate which awaits those who believe not the gospel.*
>
> —General Booth, Founder, Salvation Army

**10.** When people avoid or reject God and His involvement in their lives, do you think they realize that they are actually choosing hell? On a more personal level, why have *you* resisted God at times in your life?

**STRAIGHT TALK**

### THE FINE IS PAID

Cliffe Knechtle tells the following story:

Two close friends graduated from college in Australia. One became a judge and the other a banker. One day the banker was arrested for embezzlement of one million dollars. He was

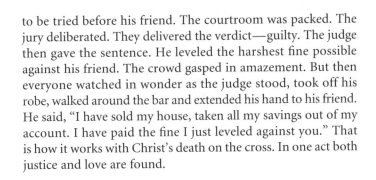

to be tried before his friend. The courtroom was packed. The jury deliberated. They delivered the verdict—guilty. The judge then gave the sentence. He leveled the harshest fine possible against his friend. The crowd gasped in amazement. But then everyone watched in wonder as the judge stood, took off his robe, walked around the bar and extended his hand to his friend. He said, "I have sold my house, taken all my savings out of my account. I have paid the fine I just leveled against you." That is how it works with Christ's death on the cross. In one act both justice and love are found.

**11.** Can hell, God's justice, and God's love all be true? Explain.

### *Charting Your Journey*

Check the statement(s) below which best describes your position at this point. Give reasons for your response.

_____ I see no reason to believe that a place called hell exists.

_____ Maybe hell exists, but it can't really be forever.

_____ I am still unsure how I feel about hell.

_____ The idea of hell bothers me because I am unsure if I will end up there or not.

_____ I am unable to reconcile the thought of a loving God condemning someone to hell.

_____ I believe that hell exists, and I am grateful that God has given us a way out.

_____ I believe that hell as described in the Bible exists.

_____ The worst thing about hell would be separation from God.

_____ I don't think hell is anything to worry about.

_____ It bothers me that there may be friends and family of mine who may wind up in hell.

_____ Other: _____

# Is There Really a Heaven?

### A Nice Place to Visit?

The way it's portrayed in the popular mind-set, heaven appears to be a bland, banal place—a sea of harp-players donned in white robes, choirs of angels singing incessantly. If this sort of sanitized setting is our eternal home, most of us wonder which would be worse: a painless, boring heaven, or a painful but interesting hell.

How can we be sure there is some kind of existence beyond death? Is there evidence we can trust? It seems lots of people want to be in heaven only because they don't want to risk hell. If all of the less than legitimate thrills of life are taken away, is the result a fleecy, feather-filled forever?

> To believe that consciousness can survive the wreck of the brain is like believing that 70 mph can survive the wreck of the car.
>
> —Frank Zindler

Maybe all this life-after-death stuff is a myth—like the Easter bunny and nursery rhymes. We tell our children stories about heaven, but we know we really don't have any solid basis for such fables. Maybe when we die, we die, and that's it. Or, if there is an afterlife, it won't be at all like what we've imagined. Besides, if we all have such differing concepts of what a great forever would look like, how can heaven hope to meet all our varied expectations? Can we even know what it will be like?

So often, people point to rewards in the afterlife as if heaven makes up for all we've had to endure here on earth. Isn't that just a way to cope? And does heaven really get God off the hook for all the pain that's happened down here? It sounds like heaven was invented to help people justify life's frustrations and God's failures. If we put all our hope in something that can't be seen, we're betting everything—and I mean everything—on a long shot. That just doesn't make sense.

In this session, we will explore reasons for believing in an afterlife and get a clearer picture of why the Bible teaches heaven is real and important.

> I would love to believe that when I die I will live again, that some thinking, feeling, remembering part of me will continue. But as much as I want to believe that, and dispute the ancient and worldwide cultural traditions that assert an afterlife, I know of nothing to suggest that it is more than wishful thinking.
>
> —Carl Sagan

> Although I cannot believe that the individual survives the death of his body, feeble souls harbor such thought through fear or ridiculous egotism.
>
> —Albert Einstein

## Open for Discussion

**1.** Do you believe that there is some kind of life after death? What reasons do you have for your answer?

> No deity will save us, we must save ourselves. Promise of immortal salvation or fear of eternal damnation are both illusory and harmful.
>
> —Humanist Manifesto II

> Convinced that there is no eternal life awaiting him, man will strive all the more to brighten his life on earth and rationally improve his condition in harmony with that of his fellows.
>
> —Ernst Haeckel

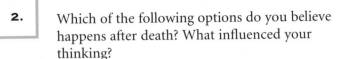

**2.** Which of the following options do you believe happens after death? What influenced your thinking?

- Nothing
- Heaven or hell
- Reincarnation
- Nirvana
- Other: _____

**3.** Which of the items listed below describe concerns you've had as you've thought about heaven?

- Will it be boring?
- Is it just wishful thinking—does it even exist?
- Will we be able to recognize people?
- Will it be sad if every loved one isn't there?
- Will we become angels with halos and wings?
- Isn't eternity a long time to be at the same place?
- Other concerns: _____

> *It goes on all day long and every day, during a stretch of twelve hours. The singing is of hymns alone, nay, it is of one hymn alone. The words are always the same; in number they are only about a dozen; there is no rhyme, there is no poetry . . .*
>
> —Mark Twain, on music in heaven

**4.** When He talked of heaven to His disciples, Jesus said, "In my Father's house are many rooms; if it were not so, I would have told you. I am going there to prepare a place for you. And if I go and prepare a place for you, I will come back and take you to be with me that you also may be where I am" (John 14:2–3). What do the phrases "many rooms" and "prepare a place" convey to you about the personal touches and loving concern Jesus says await you in heaven? How might this teaching address fears about heaven being boring?

> *In heaven there is no beer; that's why we drink it here.*
> —Words to a famous drinking song

> *Our experience on earth makes it difficult for us to apprehend a good without a catch in it somewhere.*
> —Charles Williams

**5.** Some people believe heaven is the place for those who do good and hell is the place for those who do bad. If we have to be good to enter heaven, how good do we have to be? Can anyone know for sure if he or she has been good enough?

> *The only ultimate way to conquer evil is to let it be smothered within a willing, living, human being. When it is absorbed there, like blood in a sponge or a spear thrown into one's heart, it loses its power and goes no further.*
>
> —Gale D. Webbe, *The Night and Nothing*

> *He himself bore our sins in his body on the tree, so that we might die to sins and live for righteousness; by his wounds you have been healed.*
>
> —1 Peter 2:24

**6.** According to your understanding of the Bible, on what basis do sinful people gain entrance into heaven? Do you believe people can be confident that they're going to heaven? Why or why not?

> *Here is a trustworthy saying that deserves full acceptance: Christ Jesus came into the world to save sinners. . . .*
>
> —1 Timothy 1:15

### Heart of the Matter

**7.** How confident are you that you will spend eternity in heaven? What is the basis behind that confidence (or lack thereof)?

> *And this is the testimony: God has given us eternal life, and this life is in his Son. He who has the Son has life; he who does not have the Son of God does not have the life. I write these things to you who believe in the name of the Son of God so that you may know that you have eternal life.*
>
> —1 John 5:11-13

**8.** What difference does it make to have assurance now about where you'll spend eternity?

### GOD AND PAIN

If heaven is the place where there is no pain and suffering, what are we to make of our hardships now? What is God's attitude toward our plight? Consider these insights from various observers:

The Bible never belittles disappointment. . .but it does add one key word: temporary (Philip Yancey, *Disappointment with God*).

Where is God when it hurts? He is in *you*, the one hurting, not in *it*, the thing that hurts (Dr. Paul Brand and Philip Yancey, *Pain: The Gift Nobody Wants*).

I feel free to curse the unfairness of life and to vent all my grief and anger. But I believe God feels the same way. . ..We tend to think, "Life should be fair because God is fair." But God is not life. And if I confuse God with the physical reality of life. . .then I set myself up for crashing disappointment ("Douglas," quoted in *Disappointment with God*).

**9.** Although God doesn't promise you freedom from pain in this life, is it enough that He offers to be with you now, and care for you forever in a place totally void of evil and suffering called heaven? Why or why not?

*The city does not need the sun or the moon to shine on it, for the glory of God gives it light. . . . The nations will walk by its light. . . . Nothing impure will ever enter it, nor will anyone who does what is shameful or deceitful, but only those whose names are written in the Lamb's book of life.*

—Revelation 21: 23–24, 27

*[Beauty and joy on earth represent] only the scent of a flower we have not found, the echo of a tune we have not heard, news from a country we have never yet visited.*

—C. S. Lewis

**10.** What is the importance of heaven in your own life and thinking at this point?

## Charting Your Journey

Check the statement(s) below which best describes your position at this point. Give reasons for your response.

_____ I believe that when we die that's it, it is all over.
_____ Even if there is a heaven, it can't be that great.
_____ Eternity in heaven won't compensate for life's troubles.
_____ I am confident that heaven exists, but I'm unsure if I'll end up there.
_____ I am sure I will wind up in heaven when I die.
_____ I believe most everyone will go to heaven.
_____ Other: _____

# For Further Reading

*The Case for Christ*, Lee Strobel
*Christianity Made Simple*, David Hewetson and David Miller
*Disappointment with God*, Philip Yancey
*Faith for the Non-religious*, Michael Green
*Finding Faith*, Andrew Knowles
*Give Me an Answer*, Cliffe Knechtle
*A Grace Disguised*, Gerald L. Sittser
*A Grief Observed*, C. S. Lewis
*Handbook of Christian Apologetics*, Peter Kreeft and Ronald
    Tacelli
*If God Is In Charge*, Steve Brown
*I'm Glad You Asked*, Ken Boa and Larry Moody
*Know What You Believe*, Paul Little
*Know Why You Believe*, Paul Little
*Letters from a Skeptic*, Dr. Gregory Boyd and Edward Boyd
*Making Life Make Sense*, Jay Kesler
*Mere Christianity*, C. S. Lewis
*Miracles*, C. S. Lewis
*The Gift of Pain*, Dr. Paul Brand and Philip Yancey
*Reasonable Faith: Christian Truth and Apologetics*, William
    Lane Craig
*Reason to Believe*, R. C. Sproul
*Scaling the Secular City*, J. P. Moreland
*Where Is God When It Hurts?* Philip Yancey
*Who Says God Created . . .*, Fritz Ridenour
*Why Believe?* C. Stephan Evans

## This resource was created to serve you.

It is just one of many ministry tools that are part of the Willow Creek Resources® line, published by the Willow Creek Association together with Zondervan Publishing House. The Willow Creek Association was created in 1992 to serve a rapidly growing number of churches from all across the denominational spectrum that are committed to helping unchurched people become fully devoted followers of Christ. There are now more than 2,500 WCA member churches worldwide.

The Willow Creek Association links like-minded leaders with each other and with strategic vision, information, and resources in order to build prevailing churches. Here are some of the ways it does that:

- **Church Leadership Conferences**—3 1/2-day events, held at Willow Creek Community Church in South Barrington, IL, that are being used by God to help church leaders find new and innovative ways to build prevailing churches that reach unchurched people.

- **The Leadership Summit**—a once-a-year event designed to increase the leadership effectiveness of pastors, ministry staff, volunteer church leaders, and Christians in business.

- **Willow Creek Resources®**—to provide churches with a trusted channel of ministry resources in areas of leadership, evangelism, spiritual gifts, small groups, drama, contemporary music, and more. For more information, call Willow Creek Resources® at 800/876-7335. Outside the US call 610/532-1249.

- *WCA News*—a bimonthly newsletter to inform you of the latest trends, resources, and information on WCA events from around the world.

- *The Exchange*—our classified ads publication to assist churches in recruiting key staff for ministry positions.

- **The Church Associates Directory**—to keep you in touch with other WCA member churches around the world.

- *WillowNet*—an Internet service that provides access to hundreds of Willow Creek messages, drama scripts, songs, videos, and multimedia suggestions. The system allows users to sort through these elements and download them for a fee.

- *Defining Moments*—a monthly audio journal for church leaders, in which Lee Strobel asks Bill Hybels and other Christian leaders probing questions to help you discover biblical principles and transferable strategies to help maximize your church's potential.

For conference and membership information please write or call:

Willow Creek Association
P.O. Box 3188
Barrington, IL 60011-3188

ph: (847) 765-0070
fax: (847) 765-5046
www.willowcreek.org